Facts About the Golden Lion Tamarin

By Lisa Strattin

© 2022 Lisa Strattin

FREE BOOK

FREE FOR ALL SUBSCRIBERS

FACTS ABOUT THE
SKUNK
A PICTURE BOOK FOR KIDS

Lisa Strattin

LisaStrattin.com/Subscribe-Here

BOX SET

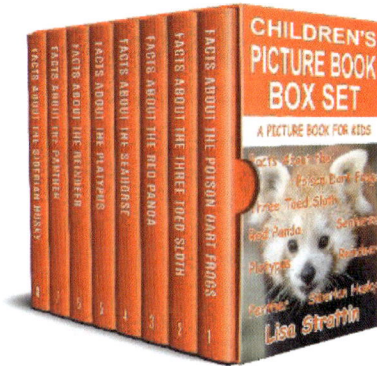

- FACTS ABOUT THE POISON DART FROGS
- FACTS ABOUT THE THREE TOED SLOTH
- FACTS ABOUT THE RED PANDA
- FACTS ABOUT THE SEAHORSE
- FACTS ABOUT THE PLATYPUS
- FACTS ABOUT THE REINDEER
- FACTS ABOUT THE PANTHER
- FACTS ABOUT THE SIBERIAN HUSKY

LisaStrattin.com/BookBundle

Facts for Kids Picture Books by Lisa Strattin

Little Blue Penguin, Vol 92

Chipmunk, Vol 5

Frilled Lizard, Vol 39

Blue and Gold Macaw, Vol 13

Poison Dart Frogs, Vol 50

Blue Tarantula, Vol 115

African Elephants, Vol 8

Amur Leopard, Vol 89

Sabre Tooth Tiger, Vol 167

Baboon, Vol 174

Sign Up for New Release Emails Here

LisaStrattin.com/subscribe-here

★★COVER IMAGE★★

https://www.flickr.com/photos/ekilby/22464182272/

★★ADDTIIONAL IMAGES★★

https://www.flickr.com/photos/wwarby/3278214221/

https://www.flickr.com/photos/cuatrok77/10600804235/

https://www.flickr.com/photos/lara604/1797207472/

https://www.flickr.com/photos/bartvandorp/14049887984/

https://www.flickr.com/photos/sherseydc/729358167

https://www.flickr.com/photos/peterkaminski/26295840434/

https://www.flickr.com/photos/vintage_illustration/51129518055/

https://www.flickr.com/photos/15016964@N02/5893808871/

https://www.flickr.com/photos/_pavan_/27617881620/

https://www.flickr.com/photos/marfis75/51864286104/

Contents

INTRODUCTION

Roar! The Golden Lion Tamarin is an endangered primate native to South America known for their resemblance to a lion's mane. Their beautiful red-gold coat and long mane are part of their signature look. They also have long, slender fingers and claws which they use to explore into narrow cracks and spaces to reach food objects.

The Golden Lion Tamarin is a highly social species, living in groups of two to eight, usually made up of family members, called a troop. The groups include a breeding pair, their offspring of possibly one or two litters, and sometimes other relatives. They spend the majority of their time in the trees, leaping, running, and jumping from branches using both their hands and feet.

CHARACTERISTICS

Golden Lion Tamarins are commonly called "squirrel-like" due to their ability to climb and jump through tree branches like squirrels. However, they are also about the same size as squirrels as well. You can't miss their characteristic bright orange fur and mane that frames their expressive faces.

They move through the trees using their hands and feet, grabbing the vines and branches, which help provide easy pathways in the trees and protection from predators from both the air and ground. The also sleep in the trees, usually in holes in the trees.

They will scent-mark their territory by rubbing their chests and behinds on underlying layers in their area, which releases an oily, musky scent. They are territorial and will defend their territory. Watch out for signs of aggression like an open mouth, arched back, and staring, as well as vocalized threats.

Since these tamarins are social, they form very strong pair bonds, with mostly equal dominance between the male and female in the family group. They also groom each other like other primates and young tamarins will play by chasing and wrestling with each other. They are diurnal, which means they are active during the day and sleep during the night; they often take a nap during the midday.

APPEARANCE

The Golden Lion Tamarin is known for their mane and orange-red fur. Their mane covers their ears and frames their dark face. They have long narrow hands and feet; long, sharp canine teeth, and short incisor teeth.

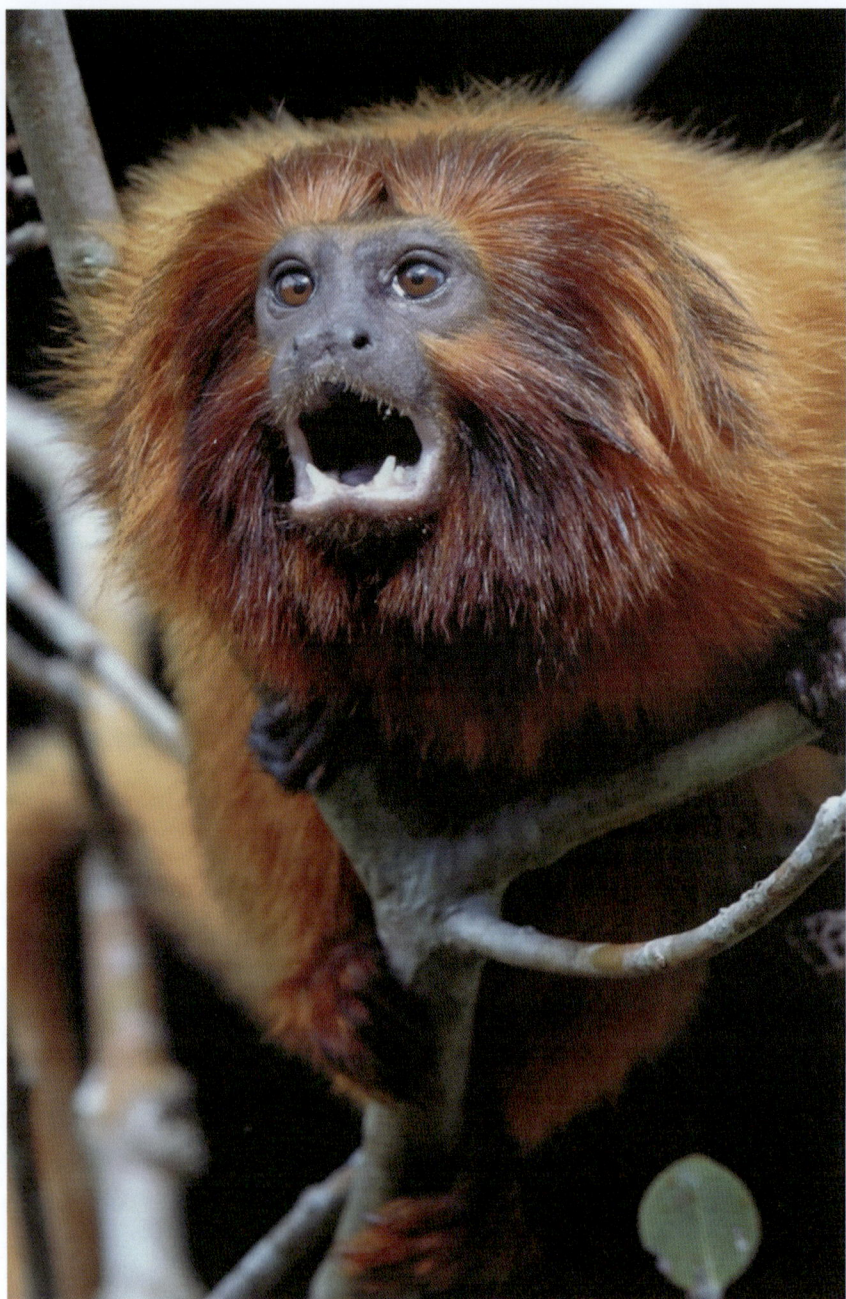

LIFE STAGES

In the wild, Golden Lion Tamarins generally live in groups between 2-9, with only one breeding pair in the group, with subadults, juveniles, and infants. Both males and females will leave the group around the age of four in order to establish their own family groups or establish rank in other groups. Mated pairs are monogamous and usually deliver twins, although triplets and single births and quadruplets have been documented by researchers. Each baby only weighs about 10% of mom's body weight. They are born fully-furred and with their eyes open.

Mom will carry the babies for the first two weeks, and then the father carries them. He will do the largest share of caring for the babies and the mother only takes them to nurse them. However, the entire group works together to raise the offspring.

The breeding season is between September and March, which is usually the hottest and wettest time of year. The pregnancy generally lasts about just over four months. At five weeks they will start to explore on their own and will become weaned between 3 and 4 months of age. Females reach sexual maturity at 18 months of age and males are sexually mature at 2 years old.

LIFE SPAN

Life is not easy for young Golden Lion Tamarins –
one half of the infants die during their first year.
Those that live past the first year generally live up to
eight years in the wild but can live up to 20 years or
more in human care. According to the Smithsonian,
the longest lived Golden Lion Tamarin lived to 31
years old!

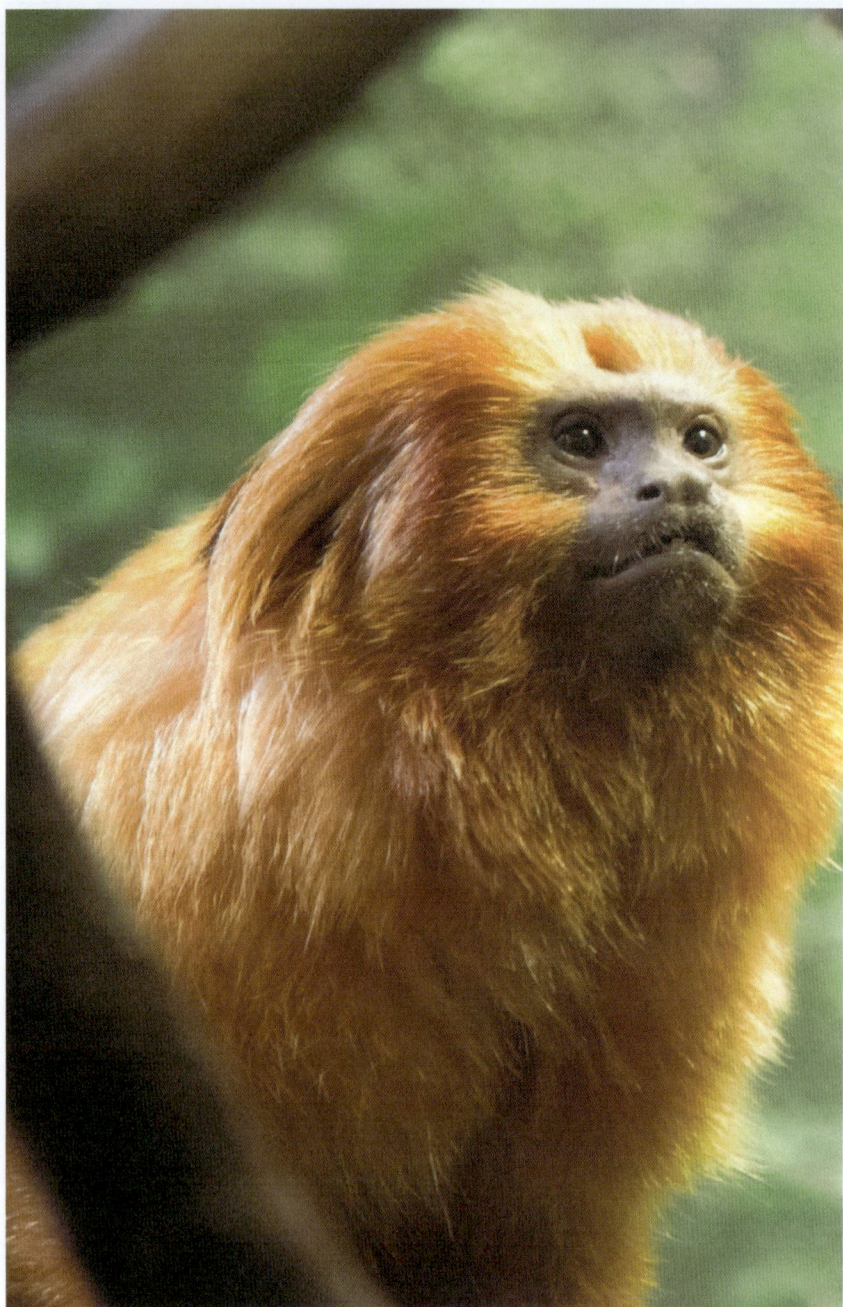

SIZE

Adults usually weigh only a pound and a half; males and females are hard to tell apart. Their head and body averages 6 to 10 inches in length and their tail adds another 12 to 15 inches.

HABITAT

Golden Lion Tamarins are found only in the Atlantic Coastal Forest, a coastal rainforest in Brazil, known as Mata Atlántico, near Rio de Janeiro. The troops generally live in a territory that averages about 100 acres in size. They live in the lowland coastal rainforest that has tangles of vines, which attracts insects and amphibians for them to eat. They stay mostly in the canopy, usually about 30-100 feet off the ground.

DIET

Golden Lion Tamarins are omnivores and eat a wide variety of foods. They like fruits, insects, and other invertebrates. They will also eat any smaller animal and bird eggs. They use their long, slender fingers to dig into cracks, bark, spiny flowers, and other hiding places for prey, like snails, small lizards, small birds, fruits and vegetables, mealworms, and crickets.

Golden Lion Tamarins will share food with their family groups, but rarely with others outside of their family. Sometimes they will actively share with the family by offering bits to others, or by passively sharing, or letting others "steal" food from them, especially if they are juveniles who are playing with their parents.

ENEMIES

Golden Lion Tamarins have several natural enemies, such as raptors and birds of prey, cats, weasels, otters, ferrets, badgers, coatis, small Brazilian wildcats, and large snakes. Tamarins give specific alarm calls in response to predators from the sky and from the ground.

SUITABILITY AS PETS

Due to their endangered status, it is illegal to own and export Golden Lion Tamarins as pets.

They are wild animals that are not cuddly, even if they are cute. It is better not to own one as a pet in order to help conserve them naturally in the wild.

You might be able to see them in your local zoo.

COLOR ME

COLOR ME

COLOR ME

COLOR ME

COLOR ME

COLOR ME

COLOR ME

COLOR ME

COLOR ME

COLOR ME

Please leave me a review here:

LisaStrattin.com/Review-Vol-469

For more Kindle Downloads Visit Lisa Strattin Author Page on Amazon Author Central

amazon.com/author/lisastrattin

To see upcoming titles, visit my website at LisaStrattin.com– most books available on Kindle!

LisaStrattin.com

FREE BOOK

FOR ALL SUBSCRIBERS – SIGN UP NOW

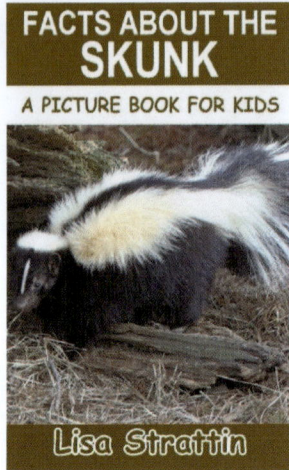

FACTS ABOUT THE
SKUNK
A PICTURE BOOK FOR KIDS

Lisa Strattin

LisaStrattin.com/Subscribe-Here

Join us on
Facebook

LisaStrattin.com/Facebook

YouTube

LisaStrattin.com/Youtube

Printed in Great Britain
by Amazon